A Love You Can Count On

A Love YOU CAN COUNT ON

A Story of Faith, Hope
and a Spare Kidney

TRACEY A. SCOTT

XULON PRESS

Xulon Press
2301 Lucien Way #415
Maitland, FL 32751
407.339.4217
www.xulonpress.com

Xulon
PRESS

Unless otherwise indicated,Scripture quotations taken from the Holy Bible,
New International Version (NIV). Copyright © 1973, 1978, 1984, 2011 by
Biblica, Inc.™. Used by permission. All rights reserved.

Printed in the United States of America.

ISBN-13: 978-1-5456-6943-3

This book is lovingly dedicated to
Jesus,
My Lord and Savior and my best friend

~

Alysha Rae,
Who asked me to write her story with the hope
that others will see God's Love

~

My husband, children, and grandchildren,
Who inspire me, love me, and make me laugh daily
They are the jewels in my crown

Contents

Prologue

Ding dong. Dingggg donggg. "I'm coming, give me a sec." It's been a while since I tried holding a toddler and, in the process, get a grip on my sweet yet incredibly strong dog, while trying to answer the door.

I open the door to see a deliveryman standing there holding a beautiful bouquet of flowers. "Oh my, give me one minute to get some order here." I set my two-year-old granddaughter, Mia, on my rocker recliner with a cookie… hoping that will keep her occupied until I can take care of the man at the door. He sees me struggling a bit and says "You can let go of your dog. I love animals."

"Oh, he'll love you, too. But in the process, he just might knock you over!"

"I can handle him," he says with a smile. "What kind of dog is he, and what's his name?"

"He's a Boxer, Mastiff, Pitt Bull mix. We rescued him in June, and we figure he's around a year old. His name is Butkus. And before you ask how we came up with that name…. I'm a big *Rocky* fan. You know the boxing movie. Anyways, his dog was named Butkus."

"Well, why don't I exchange you? You take the flowers, and I'll play with the dog."

"Ok, but remember, this was your idea." I take the flowers from him. They are in a pumpkin vase that's adorable. I pull the card out to read who they are from, but I have a pretty good idea who sent them. As I read the note, I can't help but smile.

The deliveryman notices my expression, and asks "Do you mind telling me why you're getting flowers?"

I smile even bigger, if that's possible, and am thrilled he asked. "My twenty-five-year-old daughter, Alysha Rae, sent them to me and her dad. She's in an operating room right now, donating a kidney to a family friend. The card says, 'Thank you for being the best role models and great examples of giving! Because of you, I am blessed.' That's her little girl, my granddaughter, I'm watching right now while she's in the hospital."

The man just looks at me and says, "You're kidding! She's giving a kidney and sending you flowers?"

"That's what the love of Jesus does to you. When you are filled with His love, it can't help but gush out to others!"

He looks at me and smiles back. "I knew there was something different about you. I could feel the anointing when you opened the door."

"That's one of the greatest compliments I could get. Thank you!"

He gets a bit serious on me. "Are you scared or worried?"

"Not at all. My God is mightier than anything that can come against us. I've prayed and spoken the Word over her. All is well."

"Is she really close to the person she's donating her kidney to?"

"He's been a friend for years. Alysha saw firsthand the difference a donor can make. You see, she's my middle child. My youngest child, Seanny, was diagnosed with leukemia when he was three. He had to have a lot of blood transfusions, and people donated especially for him. I knew he was healed from the beginning, but after three and a half years of chemotherapy, the doctors agreed. Later, my oldest daughter was told she had cancer when she was sixteen, but she was healed the same day. My family has been faced with a lot, but God has been good to us. He's never forsaken us. We believe freely we have received, freely we will give."

"Wow! You made my day. Now, you have a good one." He says as he starts heading back to his van.

As I am putting the flowers on the table, I can't help but notice the beauty of them. God sure is an amazing artist. "Thank you, God, for my daughter and for sharing your beautiful creation with me."

I go back to my living room. "Well, Mia Moo, it's about time for your nap." My granddaughter's name is Amelia Rae, but we call her Mia Moo, or sometimes we call her Mia Mooberry as her Uncle Seanny affectionately calls her. She reaches up for me and gives me a smile that takes up her entire face. Oh, how I love this little girl. "I bet you miss your Momma, but Grammy will take good care of you until she can."

I take her to the bedroom that Sean and I made for the grandkids. As I lay her down in the car bed, I give her a great big kiss and tell her I'll see her in a little bit. She says, "Woove you, Grammy," as she closes her eyes. My heart feels like it could explode at this moment for how incredibly blessed I am.

I go back downstairs and plop into my big, comfy rocking chair. My mind can't quit thinking about how I got to this day and how amazingly good God has been to us. I am a very organized, detailed thinker who loves the significance of numbers. As my mind goes back in time, I can't help but think this way.

Chapter 1

One. I remember the one trip Alysha and I made to Florida back in February of 2014. This wasn't the normal "mother-daughter" trip most people take. God had placed on my heart for days to go and pray for a man I didn't even know. His extended family went to my church and had put him on our prayer chain. He was in his fifties and was diagnosed with terminal cancer. Now, I love praying for people in the privacy of my home, but I didn't go out of my way very often to pray with people. Ok, so do you want to know the real catch about this? He lived in Florida, and I lived in Pennsylvania—a four-teen-hour drive apart! Weren't there any Christians in Florida who could pray with him!? The furthest drive I had ever made was three and a half hours to see a play in Lancaster, Pennsylvania... and it was in the same state. I have a horrible sense of direction and get lost very easily.

Oh, and let's not forget my bank account. I didn't even have six hundred dollars in it. So of course, I clued God in on all of this. I figured if I told Him all these issues, He'd realize He chose the wrong person. I was desperate for Him to ask someone else. After not sleeping for three nights because of the conviction I was feeling, I started feeling like Jonah from the Bible. I was running away from God's calling. God told me I was more like Moses because of all the excuses. *Ughh, fine, I'll go.* But, like Gideon, I laid out some fleeces. First, my husband had to be okay with me going. HA... I knew Sean would think I was crazy and may never see me again due to my poor sense of direction. So, on Wednesday evening, I said to him, "Hey Sean, I'm going to Florida Friday evening after work. I'll be back Sunday afternoon. God wants me to go pray with someone who lives there." What was his response? "Okay, have fun." What? This was totally out of character for him. He would never tell me I couldn't go, but he'd strongly encourage me not to. I couldn't believe he was okay with it. Humph. Alysha Rae, who was twenty-one years old at the time, volunteered to ride along. Problem with that is Alysha has as bad a sense of direction as me. Still, it was better than getting lost alone. No one outside of my immediate family knew about this trip.

So, after Alysha and I were done with work Friday evening, we were off to Florida. We left around 6:00 p.m. that evening, and I must admit we were both nervous and excited. I told her we'd eat once a day and stop as little as possible. We had "church" in my car the whole ride down. We prayed, listened to Bible teaching CDs, and praised and worshipped God for hours. We were on a spiritual high. By the thirteenth hour, we were getting a little tense and tired. The car wasn't very fresh at this point, and the ride seemed to take forever. When we finally pulled up in front of this family's house, I got nervous. *What are we doing here? These people are going to think I'm nuts... or from some cult!* "God, did I really hear you right?"

I didn't want to get out of the car. I knew why God put on Alysha's heart to go with me. She said, "Mom, we just drove fourteen hours. You barely stopped to even let me go to the bathroom. Don't make me get you out of this car!" I looked at her, trying to decide whether or not to take that challenge. She volunteered to knock on their door, so I conceded. The man's wife was a little skeptical at first, but she went to get her husband. He looked like he was in the last stages of cancer. I had planned on sharing so many healing scriptures and testimonies with him, but when I opened my mouth, what came out surprised even me. I said, "I just drove fourteen hours to tell you God loves you." That's all I said. Alysha looked at me like, "Really?!" After a moment, this man started to cry. He said he told God and his wife last night that if God didn't prove He still loved him, his life was over. He wasn't living any longer. His wife started to cry, then I did, and so did

Alysha. The depths of God's love overwhelmed all of us. God had orchestrated the whole trip and meeting with the most perfect timing, seeing to every little detail. He knew what this man needed more than anything, and that was to know God loved him. He couldn't receive anything from God until he realized just how much Jesus loved him, period.

This man experienced God's love in a way he never had before. I could see now why we had to go. There would have been no sacrifice for a neighbor to walk across the street to tell him God loved him. But for a stranger to drive fourteen hours one way, with the sole purpose of giving that message, was just miraculous. We felt so humbled and honored that God asked us to be a part of this miracle. We could see the whole picture now, and we realized God never does anything randomly or without a plan. Another miracle about this story – we never got lost, not even once.

So, after visiting with this man for about an hour, we got back into my car and headed to Pennsylvania. We thought we were on a "high" on the trip down, but we were completely overwhelmed and floating on the trip home.

This man's nephew sent us a text message that I keep framed on my desk. It says, "Thank you for your radical love. Your obedience to God is inspiring. What you did in 20 minutes preached a thousand sermons. It was a game changer."

One. We saw firsthand how God always goes after the one. The one is just that important. The one is just that loved.

Chapter 2

⤳

Two. Bruce Bandel had kidney failure for two years. Two years he was believing God for a divine miracle. For two years, God was listening and working everything out.

My family had known Bruce's family before I was even born. My dad worked for his dad at the local post office. Then my grandfather lived on the Bandel farm where he helped take care of it. I myself spent a lot of time on that farm because Bruce's sister and I were very close friends, she was even in my wedding. Bruce was much older than his sister, so he was married and living elsewhere when I hung out on the farm. None the less, the Bandels and my family were very close.

My husband loves cars; he is borderline obsessive about it. Bruce's brother, Greg, owns a used car dealership that Sean visited frequently. When they got together, they talked about all their old muscle cars. Greg had a couple of old Corvettes, and Sean had old Chevys. Bruce would go to his brother's shop, and if Sean was there, they would talk about cars for hours. Bruce owned old Corvettes, Camaros, and even a Nova. When Sean started drag-racing, Bruce and Greg would occasionally show up to cheer him on.

The most important thing we had in common with Bruce was our faith. We all loved Jesus so much. Bruce was a pastor and even had his own church for years. Then he started attending the same church as us. He married my oldest daughter, Brittini, and her husband, Ray. Their wedding was part of the show *Four Weddings* that was on TLC. So, Bruce was on tv with them. On a side note, Brittini and Ray's wedding came in first place, so they won a free honeymoon to Puerto Rico. God loves to bless His children.

Bruce was a very fun, enthusiastic guy who has the energy of someone half his age. He was always laughing and carrying on about something. He and his wife threw some very fun, memorable parties. Bruce was the type of guy that if you were looking for someone to do something with, you called him. He was up for about anything. His enthusiasm was contagious. He truly knew how to enjoy life and all the blessings God gave him.

Around Christmas time in 2016, Bruce got a phone call he would never forget. He was at a Christmas party when his phone rang. He saw that it was his primary care physician. He had been seeking medical help with a prostate condition and figured that's what the call was about. The doctor urged him to go to the emergency room immediately. The prostate problem had affected his kidneys. At the hospital, they did blood work and other tests. The results revealed that life-threatening damage had been done. His kidneys were no longer working.

Over the next two years, Bruce was in and out of the hospital and on dialysis. He lived life as fully as he could, but his body was limiting him. Everything that he was going through was taking a hard toll on his body. He never gave up believing for his miracle, though. He knew his God and never doubted that it was God's will to heal him.

I believe with my whole heart that God loves to heal... it's in His nature. God has seven redemptive names that reveal who He is. One of those names is Jehovah Rapha, which means the God who heals. It's part of who He is. I also believe God uses different methods to heal. Throughout the Gospels, Jesus heals anyone who comes to Him in faith. He never said no, not even once. Sometimes He would touch the person and heal them. Other times He would speak the Word and heal them. He even used mud and spit to heal others. Bottom line, He is the healer, no matter what method is used. He meets us where we are and works with us from there. He doesn't force healing or salvation on anyone, but it's always ours for the taking.

Jesus paid the price and took the curse of sickness for us. It says in Isaiah 53:5, "But He was wounded for our transgressions, He was crushed for our iniquities; the punishment that brought us peace was on Him, and by His wounds we are healed." Those are shouting words! Jesus paid the price by having His back whipped and torn apart. He didn't even look human after this beating. He did this to pay, actually overpay, for every curse of sickness, disease, and pain we would ever face. He gave us the victory over this. Wow! This just makes me give Him my endless hallelujah.

Two. Two years, Bruce cried out to God for a healing. Two years Bruce and his family trusted that God heard and was answering them. Two years God was working in Alysha's life and on her heart to prepare her for being a part of this miracle. Two years God was lining everything up perfectly to make this happen.

Chapter 3

Three. Alysha had three miscarriages between 2013 and 2018. Three times her heart was shattered and broken for the children she longed to hold. Three times she had to trust God to take care of her children until she gets to Heaven.

From the time Alysha was two years old, she wanted to be a mom. That dream never died or changed. She would play with her baby dolls like they were her real kids. She would talk to them, sing them "Jesus Love Me," feed them, and take care of them. As she got older, she took every babysitting job available. She just loved being around children. She was destined to be a mother.

Alysha married "the one her soul loves" on August 17, 2013. Chris and Alysha knew they wanted a family immediately. They both had a strong desire to have children and saw no reason to wait.

The fall after they were married, Alysha's period was late. So, one Thursday afternoon in late September, she secretly went to Wal-Mart to buy a pregnancy test. She came home, rushed to the bathroom, and took the test. After waiting the required two minutes, which seemed like two hours, there was a plus sign in the window. She was pregnant. She wanted to shout it from the mountain-tops, but she also wanted to make this a special occa-sion for Chris. She had read about so many different ways that wives surprised their husbands with the news, she wanted to do the same. She made plans to tell him that Sunday. She would place the pregnancy test in Chris's man cave with a little baby onesie that said "Daddy's favorite" on it. She was so excited she could hardly stand it. Saturday afternoon, after working that morning, Alysha came home and started putting laundry away. Suddenly, the mother of all cramps overwhelmed her. She could barely stand. She made her way to the bathroom and real-ized she was bleeding profusely. She hollered for Chris and told him she thought she was having a miscarriage. He was shocked, "What? You think you're pregnant? How do you know?" Between cramps and pain, she said, "I took a test." He responded, "Oh my gosh, what do you need me to do?" As she laid there on the bathroom floor, she didn't know which hurt worse, her stomach or her broken dream. "There's nothing you can do. I don't want to go to the ER; we don't have health insurance. Let's not tell anyone." But there was a crack left in their hearts that no one but God knew about.

Two years went by, and Alysha and Chris decided to try again to have a baby. They didn't mind the "trying" part at all... smile. After months of anticipation, their work paid off. Six days before their second anniversary, Alysha bought another pregnancy test. Lo and behold, Alysha was pregnant again. Chris decided to celebrate their anniversary a day early by taking her to dinner. She asked Chris if he wanted his gift first, and of course, he said, "Yes!" He opened his gift, which was an Eddie Bauer backpack. The note read, "This is for our next big adventure." Inside of the backpack was a positive pregnancy test and some baby clothes. He was so excited that he started waving the test stick around. Alysha said, "You know I peed on that thing, right?!" He laughed as he hugged her tightly.

They decided to surprise Sean and I on Sean's birthday. They bought baby cowboy boots and went to the barn where I kept my horse. They put the boots on a bale of hay. They had my horse, Trooper, stand beside it, and put up a sign that said, "My new rider is due next April." They took a picture of this and put it inside of a birthday card. So, on August 19, 2015, we went to Buffalo Wild Wings to celebrate Sean's birthday. When he opened Alysha's card, he had no idea what he was looking at. He showed me, and I immediately knew we were going to have another grandchild! We were all so excited; it was by far Sean's favorite gift.

Alysha had already been to her eight-week appointment and was already scheduled for her twelve-week appointment. She was feeling good and getting more excited each day. Ten weeks into the pregnancy, I got a call at the school where I taught kindergarten. They paged me to come to the secretary's desk where I answered the phone. It was Alysha. She asked if she could pick me up, so I could go to the outpatient clinic because she needed to have an ultrasound done. Alysha proceeded to tell me that she had been spotting for ten days, and the doctor wanted to run some tests. I could sense the fear that was trying to grip Alysha. I silently prayed for my daughter. When we got there, they took us back to a room to do an ultrasound. You could see the concerned look on the technician's face. She didn't say much in front of Alysha...she didn't have to. When Alysha left the room, the technician said to me, "There is no heart beat or baby. Just the yoke sac where the baby should be." My heart sank. I didn't know what to say to Alysha. As we were walking down the stairs, I could tell she was struggling to keep it together. As her mother, I was feeling what she was. I told her quietly, "It's okay to cry. Even Jesus did." Between broken sobs she said, "I'm okay." Then the floodgates opened and the tears fell. I tried so hard to be strong for her, but I could feel a tear falling down my own cheek.

Alysha refused to speak death. She held on to the hope that everything was okay. A few days later, Chris and Alysha decided to go to Magee Hospital because she was still bleeding. They told her she must have miscalculated her due date because the baby was only six weeks along. There was no heartbeat because you can't detect that until eight weeks. Hope sprang into full life in their hearts. She called and told me the news, and we rejoiced together.

Later that same night, I got a call from Alysha to come to the local emergency room. I arrived around 11:00 p.m. and rushed back to where Alysha was. She was moaning in pain, and there was blood everywhere. I asked what was going on. They told me they did an ultrasound, and although they found the baby, she was in the process of a miscarriage. They said it was inevitable. They tried to give Alysha some pain medication, but she refused. She said as long as the baby was in her, she would treat it as if it were alive. Chris was beside himself. He hated seeing Alysha this way. He had just started a new job, so I told him it wasn't a good idea to call off. I told him to go to work, and I'd take Alysha home with me. For the next five days, Alysha wouldn't stop bleeding. Alysha had to be rushed back to the emergency room where she definitely had a miscarriage. They scheduled her for a D&C the next day. D&C stands for Dilation and Curettage. This is a procedure where a surgeon must open the cervix and scrape or vacuum the uterus. They didn't want anything to remain in her because that could cause a serious infection. The crack in her heart just got longer and wider. Only her Creator could fix it at this point.

A few years passed, and Alysha's dream of being a mother grew instead of breaking. She wanted a child so badly. Satan whispered words of doubt and anger in her soul, words like, "Isn't it ironic that drug addicted mothers have no problem having children they don't even want? Why won't God give you one?" Although these words stabbed at her heart, they didn't destroy her. She knew these were lies from the enemy that were meant to make her bitter. But she had a dream and a God who would fulfill it.

Sunday, April 1, 2018 was Easter. My oldest daughter, Brittini, and her family lived in Virginia. Her husband was a Lieutenant in the Air Force, and this was where he was currently stationed. They had a three-year-old boy, my grandson, whose name is Judah. His name means, "Praise God!" Unfortunately, they couldn't come home and celebrate with us. So, Alysha and her family, my son, Seanny, and Sean and myself went to church to celebrate the resurrection of Jesus. Alysha had invited us to have lunch at her place after church. After eating a huge and delicious meal, we went to the living room to relax. As we were sitting there, Mia came out of her bedroom wearing a sticker that said, "Promoted to Big Sister." I looked at

Alysha incredulously and said, "Is this an April Fool's joke?" She laughed and said, "No...I'm really pregnant!" I was so excited for them. I asked her if she had been to the doctor yet. She said they couldn't get her in until the end of April. By that time, she would be eleven weeks along.

The following week, I sent Alysha flowers to congratulate her on being pregnant. She was so excited she was bursting at the seams. Every time we talked, she told me something new about the baby. She couldn't decide how to decorate the nursery, but I reassured her she had some time before she had to make the final decision. I was already thrilled about having another grandbaby, but Alysha's excitement was contagious.

Towards the end of April, Alysha started spotting some. She was worried but didn't want to speak negatively. Late on the night of April 29, Alysha and Chris went to the emergency room. She was bleeding a lot by this time and didn't know what to do. After doing an ultrasound, the baby was only measuring six weeks old, and there was no heartbeat. Her hormone levels were dropping, which confirmed she was in the process of miscarrying. They told her to go home and her body would take care of everything naturally. Alysha was just numb but went to work the next day. By Wednesday, Alysha was fevered and in a lot of pain. She left work and headed to the emergency room yet once again. Come to find out her body didn't naturally take care of it, and they had to do another

D&C. They told her that she had lost a son. Knowing this made her mourn in a deeper way. How was her heart ever supposed to recover losing three children? Each tear Alysha cried filled my heart with sadness. As her mother, I wanted to fix everything. I wanted to somehow take her pain and carry it myself. But that's not how life works. Only God could restore us. Alysha needed to mourn, and she needed to heal.

Three. Some say Alysha lost three children... but they're not lost. We know exactly where they are and who they are with. Three times she had to turn the pieces over to God and allow Him to put her back together. Three times she emerged stronger than she ever realized.

Chapter 4

Four. Four times Alysha was pregnant, yet she only had three miscarriages. Between her second and third miscarriages, something happened. Something that most said was impossible. Most don't know that our God specializes in the impossible.

In December 2015, after her second miscarriage, Alysha started seeing a chiropractor who specialized in fertility. Alysha really liked this doctor because she took the time to listen and work with her. After taking x-rays and reviewing her CT scans, the doctor told Alysha her uterus was tilted and her body needed some major adjustments. Alysha already knew her uterus was backwards, and her OB-GYN doctor told her she had a 30% or less chance of carrying a baby full term. For two months, Alysha visited this chiropractor and prayed. After her appointment on February 16, 2016, Alysha decided to stop at the local Rite-Aid and buy a pregnancy test. Hope was stirring in her, and she couldn't wait to get home and take the test. As she waited three hours for the results...ok, it was only two minutes, her mind raced. It's amazing how many thoughts can cross through your mind in two short minutes. When the time was up, she looked at the test. There was a plus sign. She was pregnant. She sat down and thanked God. She asked Him to protect this child and to let her carry it full term. Then she started thinking of ways to tell her husband. As she was planning, her phone rang. She answered it, and it was Chris. He was telling her what a hard and bad day he had at work. He sounded so down and discouraged. She couldn't contain herself another minute. "I'm pregnant," she blurted out. In that second, Chris went from having a horrible day, to one of the best days of his life. He was through-the-roof excited. He stopped at Chick-fil-A on his way home because it was Alysha's favorite place to eat. When he walked through their door, he handed Alysha two chocolate chip cookies—one for her and one for the baby.

At this point, Alysha was working as my aid at a Christian school where I taught kindergarten. We enjoyed our class and had a lot of fun working together. It was March, and I was planning a family vacation for that September to honor my husband retiring from the Pennsylvania State Police. We had never taken a family vacation before, but we were at the point that we finally could. Sean had been a Trooper for twenty-five years. He had seen the ugly side of life and how inhumane people could truly be. Police give a whole new definition to the verse, "No greater love has a man than this, than to lay down his life for his friends" (John 15:13). Police are willing to lay down their lives for complete strangers, with little or no gratitude from those they help. I wanted to show him how proud we were of him, so I was renting a house for the whole family in Florida for an entire week.

As we were in our classroom waiting for the students to arrive, Alysha says out of nowhere, "I don't think I can go on vacation with the family the last week of September."

"Why not? I figured you would enjoy this vacation more than anyone else. You've never got to fly before or see the beach." I couldn't fathom why someone would pass up a free vacation.

"I'm pregnant and due in October. I don't think it's a good idea to travel that far eight and a half months pregnant."

I just looked at her. A smile creeps over my face and I admit, "I thought you were! Congratulations! Are you sure you don't want to come along...there are hospitals in Florida you know?"

She laughs and says, "No, I'll be more comfortable being close to my doctors. You just better be prepared to have to fly back quick if I go into labor early!"

I was so happy for her I could have just burst. Very quietly, I could hear the voice of the enemy saying, "It's just like the last two times. Alysha will never carry a baby more than a couple of months. Don't get too excited. You're her mother; don't allow her to get her hopes up."

From having a close personal relationship with God, I could tell the difference between His voice and Satan's. It says in John 10:10, "The thief comes to steal, kill and destroy. I have come that you might have life and have it abundantly." Then it says in James 1:17, "Every good and perfect gift is from above, coming down from the Father..." So, it's really simple to distinguish what voice you're hearing in your head. Is it good, loving, and encouraging? Then it's from God. Is it fearful, hurtful, or condemning? Then it's from Satan. It's not complicated or confusing. God made it clear and easy to understand.

As this voice continued to speak fearful and worrisome thoughts, I had to make a choice quickly. I could get into agreement with those words, or I could rebuke it and replace it with the Word of God. I took my God-given authority and declared, "Alysha, I'm so excited for you and can't wait to hold my new grandchild. We're going to have so much fun together." By speaking those words, I was doing battle. I was drawing a line that I just dared Satan to try to cross. Satan fears a child of God who knows the Word and how to use it. Our words have the power of life or death according to Proverbs 18:21. Satan wasn't taking this child. I made a decision right then not to speak any words about this baby unless they were good and full of life.

A month went by, and our family decided to go visit Brittini and her family in Virginia. Judah was celebrating his first birthday on March 27th, and we all wanted to be there. We had such a great time being together and loving on Judah. Sean, Seanny, and I left the next day. Alysha and Chris decided to stay a little bit longer. While she was there, Alysha started spotting. Concern overwhelmed her. Every time she went to the bathroom and saw the blood, she thanked God for protecting her baby. Faith doesn't look at the obvious, it looks at what the Word of God says. Faith believes before it sees the results. Faith believes the impossible.

After five days, Alysha quit bleeding. Although she was nauseated frequently, she was doing good and growing every day. Our kindergarten class had a "Show & Tell" day in April, so Alysha decided to participate. She brought in cupcakes, passed them out to the class, and told them there was a baby in her stomach that would come out when they were in first grade. The kids were so excited and full of questions. One student asked if the baby would have room for furniture in her tummy. Another boy told the class, "To get the baby out, they have to cut you from your chin to your toes!" It was so cute and enlightening to share this experience with our class. Five-year old children are quite insightful and curious... smile.

Alysha was plugging along in her pregnancy. In June, they decided to have a gender reveal party. When I was pregnant, there was no such thing as this. I found it pretty exciting that we would all learn together whether Alysha was carrying a boy or a girl. The party was at my house, and we had pink and blue decorations everywhere. When you walked in, there was one basket full of blue necklaces and another basket full of pink necklaces. You had to pick a color to decide what team you were on. Alysha picked a pink necklace, Chris took a blue one. I chose pink. Alysha had given a sealed envelope to a baker which had a note from the clinic on what sex the baby was. The baker put colored icing inside the cake that would let us know if it was a boy or girl. When the time finally came for Alysha and Chris to cut the cake, everyone crowded around to have the first look. As they pulled the first piece out... it was pink! I was having a granddaughter... oh, and Alysha was having a daughter. They had names picked out already. They decided if they were having a little girl, her name would be Amelia Rae. Perfect.

The months flew by, although I don't know if Alysha would agree. When we left for our Florida vacation in September, Alysha promised to call if she went into labor. I didn't go anywhere without my cell phone. Fortunately, I never got an emergency call to fly home.

Alysha grew bigger and bigger... and bigger. She just knew her baby was coming the first week of October. When that didn't happen, she knew the little one would come the second week. That didn't happen. She didn't come the third or fourth week either. This little one was stubborn already, just like the rest of the women in our family.

Finally, on November 1st, I got the call I'd been waiting weeks for. Alysha said her water broke shortly after midnight, and she was already at the hospital. Sean, Seanny, and I got there in record time—just so we could sit there and wait. And wait. For once, time was going so slow. Alysha didn't realize how hard it was to just sit there for such a long time... smile.

At 1:27 p.m., a cry pierced the air. A voice was heard that would change the world, especially ours. Amelia Rae McConnell came into this world weighing eight pounds and one ounce and was twenty inches long. She had a head full of black hair, and a voice so strong there was no mistaking it. And she was perfect. We thanked God for this miraculous blessing and loved her more than we realized was possible.

The next day, Sean and I went to visit our new grandbaby at the hospital. Alysha looked so good and happy. She was snuggling her daughter when we walked in. As we were talking, a nurse walked in to check on them. She asked Alysha if the baby had peed yet. Alysha checked the diaper and said, "No." The nurse informed her that if the baby didn't pee by morning, she wouldn't be allowed to go home. They would have to start running tests to see what the problem was. I could sense the fear that Alysha was trying to hide. Well, this just wasn't acceptable. I walked over to where Alysha was holding her, and I put my hand on that child and said quietly, "Mia, you are healed by the stripes of Jesus. No weapon formed against you shall prosper. Fear be gone in the name of Jesus. Mia, you pee now." Then I stepped away. After visiting for about five more minutes, the dam broke. Mia didn't just pee a little dribble... she let loose. I just smiled and said, "Thank you, Jesus."

Four. That's the number of children Chris and Alysha have. One of those children have been entrusted to their care for now, and the others are with Jesus awaiting to be with their momma and papa. Each child was a gift, and each left Alysha with a gift. The first pregnancy gave her the gift of empathy. She could relate to other people's pain and heartache in a way she never could before. The second pregnancy gave her the gift of courage. Not only had Alysha faced her fear of needles, but she realized that she could and would do whatever it took to become a mother. The third pregnancy gave her the gift of Amelia Rae, her rainbow baby. Amelia is a miracle and a child of promise. The fourth gave her the gift of boldness. After this loss, Alysha boldly told God in order for her heart to

heal, she needed to know her body could still give life...
like it was created to do. Four gifts. Together they shaped
Alysha's life into the calling God has for her... callings she
will use for the rest of her life.

Chapter 5

*F*ive. Five months of testing is what Alysha went through to donate her kidney. Five months that pushed Alysha both physically and mentally. Testing is never fun, but it shows you where your heart is and what you're really made of.

On June 19, 2018, Alysha called Allegheny General Hospital. She had gotten the number from Bruce. She needed to talk to the intake coordinating nurse about how to officially start the donation process. That first phone call lasted about a half an hour. So many questions. How do you know Bruce? Do you feel pressured to donate? What's your health history? What's your family's health history? On and on and on the questions were asked. Finally, at the end of the call, the nurse said she qualified to start the process. She set up an appointment for Alysha to be evaluated by the transplant team on July 23rd.

In the meantime, Alysha had to do a twenty-four-hour urinalysis. During this time, she had to drink a lot of liquids then collect, save, and refrigerate all her urine. The next morning, before she left to drop her urine off at the hospital, she sent me a picture. She was standing in front of her refrigerator holding two containers of pee. The caption read, "What's in your fridge?" I have to admit, I laughed about that all day. When Alysha arrived at the hospital to drop off her containers, the nurse asked, "Did you do that for more than twenty-four hours?" Alysha replied, "No." To which the nurse responded, "That's a lot of urine!" Oh my.

As she was about to leave, the nurse told her to hold on because she had to have some blood work done. It's a good thing Alysha didn't know beforehand how much blood they were about to take. From the time Alysha was a little girl, needles were her enemy. Anytime she got vaccinated, she would pass out. Then there was the time when she was twelve years old that she wanted to have her ears pierced. I took her and her brother, Seanny, to the mall store that did piercings. Alysha sat there nervously as they punched a hole in each ear. I went to the back counter to pay, when all of a sudden, I heard a crash. Seanny said when she stood up, she got woozy and fell over into the store's sign. I helped her up, even though she was about the same size as me and tried to shoulder most of her weight. Seanny was only ten at the time, so there was no way he could carry her. I got her to a nearby bench and started looking for a stand to buy her a soda. There was one about thirty feet away, so I rushed over to buy one. She took a couple of drinks, stood up, and fell flat on her back. No one stopped and offered any help. I overheard a middle-aged couple say, "Look at her, she's probably drunk." If it weren't for the fact that I would have had to leave Alysha laying in the middle of the mall... I may have gone after that couple. But Alysha needed me more, even though she wasn't aware of it (smile). I wasn't sure what to do, so I figured I was going to have to carry her. I honestly think Alysha may have weighed more than me, I only weighed ninety-five pounds at that time. I knew I could carry her, but I knew I couldn't do it gracefully. As I bent over to pick her up, someone tapped me on my shoulder. It was a security guard with a wheelchair. I hated drawing attention to us, but I figured this might be better than throwing her over my shoulder. After explaining to him what was going on, he wheeled Alysha to our Suburban. Once she got in the vehicle, she perked up and was fine. So, as you can see, Alysha did not like needles. When the nurse heard this story, she decided it was best to lay Alysha down before poking her arm. After what seemed like an eternity, Alysha asked how many tubes of blood they took, and the nurse replied, "Twenty-one." It's a good thing Alysha was lying down.

The transplant team met with Alysha on July 23rd. First, she met with two doctors and had a physical. Then she met with a social worker and a donor advocate. After that, she had another urine test, chest x-ray, and EKG done. These people were really going to know her inside and out! She found out on this day that she was a match with Bruce—a good match. This wasn't a surprise to us... God was working out all the details. He didn't place it on Alysha's heart just to find out it wouldn't work. He knew all along who would be a good match for Bruce and who would say "yes."

The next appointment was August 2nd at Children's Hospital in Pittsburgh. She had to have a GFR test done, which stands for glomerular filtration rate. They placed an IV in each of her arms, injected radioactive isotopes, then waited to draw blood intermittently for two hours to test her kidney function. Alysha never knew she could be poked so many times and live. There was absolutely nothing fun about this test.

On Friday, August the tenth, Alysha had to drive back to Pittsburgh for a CT scan followed by an evaluation with a psychologist. We teased Alysha that this would be the hardest test yet. There were so many questions. Why would you want to donate? How would you feel if your kidney is rejected by the recipient? How did having previous surgeries affect you? What was it like to go through so many miscarriages? Do you feel you are capable of coping with stressful situations? Have you ever been through any particularly stressful circumstances? Alysha's response was priceless. She answered, "I want to be a part of Bruce's miracle. If I am healthy enough and able to, I want to give Bruce and his family the best quality of life possible. I have a younger brother that was diagnosed with leukemia when he was three. He wasn't given a good prognosis. If he lived, he would have to go through three and a half years of chemotherapy. His blood counts were so bad the first year, causing him to have many blood and platelet transfusions. People came from everywhere to give blood for him. I saw firsthand how important donation was. I also saw how important it was to trust God and take Him at His Word. Once I donate my kidney, it's out of my hands and in God's. It's not for me to worry about rejection. It's my place to be obedient to what He asks me to do." She passed the psych evaluation.

Alysha was sitting in her primary care physician's office on Monday August 13th to get her final clearance from them stating she was healthy and cleared for surgery. As she sat there, she planned a small party for that evening with our family and Bruce. She hadn't seen Bruce in person since the beginning of June when this all started. He had no idea how far along in the process she was, or even if she had continued with it. She called Bruce and invited him to our house for pizza. Then she went to Giant Eagle to pick up a cake she had special ordered. That evening, when Bruce and his wife, Vicky, arrived we sat and made small talk over dinner. When Alysha brought out dessert, Bruce was speechless. It was a cake shaped like a green kidney, and she had written on it, "Urine for a Treat." Did you catch the pun? Instead of "You Are in for a Treat", it said "Urine for a Treat." Ok, it was cheesy but perfect. She proceeded to tell him that she was finished with all the testing, approved, and a match. Bruce started crying. He couldn't believe she was that far along and going through with it. He said that he had made a peace about receiving a kidney. Bruce also told God He would have to work everything out... so He did. Alysha thanked Bruce for allowing her to be a part of his miracle. She told him the hardest part for her was she couldn't pick up Mia for eight weeks. Staying with me and being with Mia was enough, though. Eight weeks would fly by. Sean and I told Vicky, "If you thought Bruce was ornery before, wait till he has some Scott in him!" It was a time of celebration and rejoicing. Bruce then prayed a prayer of thanksgiving and a special blessing over our families. There was so much love and gratitude in that room... it was just overwhelming.

The intake coordinating nurse called Alysha on August 29th. The tentative surgery date was scheduled for November 16th, with the pre-op appointment on November 5th. It was tentative for a couple of reasons. First, the surgeons had to be available. Sometimes they get called away for an emergency. Second, both her and Bruce would have to be healthy at this time. Even a cold could delay the surgery. We started declaring right then for divine health and favor to surround them.

Although all the testing was borderline torturous, it was almost easier than playing the waiting game until November. This is the time you have to focus on God and His Word, because this is the time Satan tries to play mind games. He tries to make you second guess your decision. He tries to whisper in your ear that you might not survive the surgery. He tries to convince you something is going to go wrong. This is the time he uses "well-meaning people," to tell you you're crazy and not thinking straight. This is when he will try to get you to fear. But this was the time we took our rightful authority and told fear to go back to hell. We refused to speak words of doubt and negativity. We praised and worshipped God. We stood on the promise of God for Alysha and Bruce, "With long life will God satisfy you and show you His salvation" (Psalm 91:16).

November 5th finally arrived. Chris drove Alysha to her pre-op appointment, which was a blessing because unbeknownst to Alysha... they had to do a repeat of the tests since it had been a few months. So, once again Alysha had to have a chest x-ray, an EKG, and twenty-one tubes of blood drawn. Again, she survived. Another good that came from this... Alysha's fear of needles was diminishing (smile).

The day before the surgery, Alysha and I decided to pamper ourselves a little bit and had facials done. Talk about relaxing. God knew Alysha needed this before the bowel prep she had to do that evening. If you've never done a bowel prep, you can't begin to imagine what this is like. She started drinking this thick, clear liquid around 3:00 p.m. Although the over-the-counter instructions say not to exceed more than one bottle in a twenty-four-hour period, the transplant team told her to drink two that evening. Then you wait for it to hit you... and it does! From 5:00 that evening until 3:00 a.m. the next morning, Alysha didn't leave the bathroom. Her family slept at my house that night because Mia was staying with me when they left very early in the morning. The noises we heard coming out of the bathroom from various parts of her body were frightening (hahaha). She said as hard as it was to get it down, it was even harder coming up. Then next morning when she arrived at the hospital, they asked her if she was cleaned out... and she said, "Oooh yeah!"

Five. Five months of testing and waiting Alysha went through. Five is the number of grace. And it took God's grace to get her through those months... and it was enough.

October 1998 - Alysha, Tracey, Brittini, Sean Jr,
Tracey's 28th birthday

August 17th 2013 - Chris and Alysha on their wedding day

August 2016 - Brittini, Sean Jr and Alysha on family farm

November 2nd 2016 - Alysha & Amelia in hospital

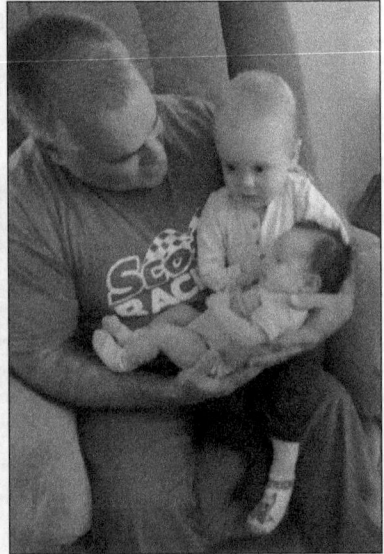

Thanksgiving 2016 - Sean Sr., Judah & Amelia Rae

February 2017- Alysha & Amelia Rae

2017- Family Picture

Tracey, Brittini, Amelia Rae & Alysha

Brittini, Alysha & Sean Jr.

November 2017 - Chris, Alysha & Amelia Rae at her 1st Birthday

June 2017 - Judah, Grammy, Pappy & Mia

July 2018 - Alysha's 24 hour urinalysis. "What's in your fridge?"

Summer 2018 - Mia, Tracey & Judah at local donut shop

August 2018 - Bruce, Alysha & Vicky. "Urine for a Treat" kidney cake

November 16th 2018 - Alysha the morning of transplant surgery

November 16th 2018 - flowers to Tracey from Alysha
on the day of surgery

Butkus & Mia snuggling

December 2018 - Famiy dinner at the Bandels

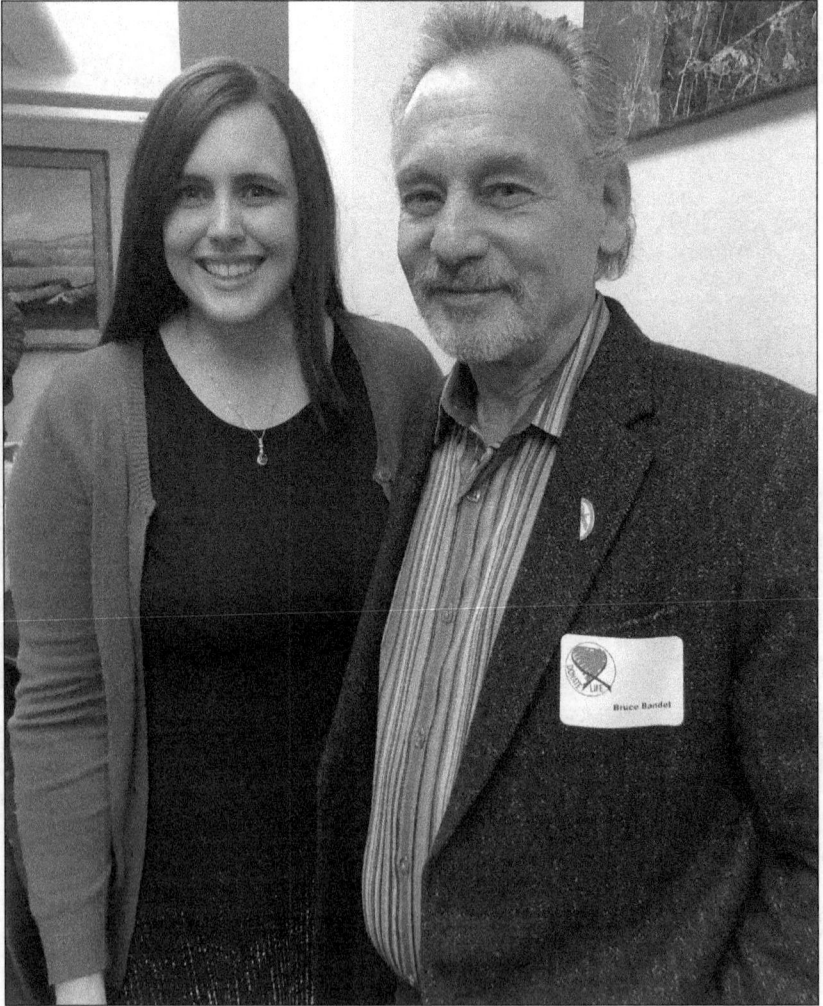

Valentines Day 2019 - Alysha & Bruce at
Donor Pinning Ceremony

Chapter 6

Six. Six different court dates our family went to from 2015 through 2018 dealing with one single trial. A trial that would change my family's lives forever. A trial Satan tried to break us with. A trial that no one should ever have to go through.

In 2014, my oldest daughter, Brittini, told me she needed to talk to me. She was twenty-three years old at the time and married. I felt something in my stomach turn at the way she said it. I could tell she was a little hesitant to talk to me, which was very unusual. She looked me in the eye and said, "Uncle Tommy raped me from the time I was six until I was eight years old." I felt like I just got sucker punched in the gut. Uncle Tommy was my older brother. She went on, "When Seanny was diagnosed with leukemia, you were at Children's Hospital a lot, and Alysha and I stayed with Grandma and Pappy. While you were gone is when he attacked me." Tommy and his family lived in half of my parents' house. Whenever my children were there, so was he. My heart was breaking. So many emotions hit me at one time, I couldn't think straight. I was crushed, sad, angry, hurt, mad, and broken. I tried hard not to let these emotions show as Brittini continued talking to me. "At the age of six, I didn't know what rape was. It stopped after Seanny got better and you were home all the time. I have reason to believe he is still sexually assaulting girls. I need to press charges... not only for the sake of justice, but to stop him. If I don't, I'll feel responsible for everyone he continues to hurt." I couldn't believe what I was hearing. At one of the weakest, hardest moments of my family's life... my brother attacked my little girl. It took her years to be able to talk about it. I told her I'd always have her back and be there for her. I didn't know what else to say. Sorry seemed so insufficient and small.

She went to the police and filed a report. There was another girl that came forward, too, and pressed charges. I admired their guts. It started a very long and grueling process. The police had to do an investigation and collect as much incriminating evidence as possible. Brittini and her family lived in Virginia at this time, so they had some distance from the onslaught of people's foolishness. Alysha had to let the police in the farmhouse to search through my brother's stuff. He was living in Texas at this time but had left a lot of his possessions at my mom's. Chris and Alysha lived in a trailer on the farm, which was next door to my mother's house. Late at night, people would drive by and scream my brother's name and say vulgar things. Didn't they realize he wasn't even there? Many nights Alysha felt unsafe because she was never sure how far these angry people would go. If they had only realized how much they were affecting innocent people.

My brother was subpoenaed and turned himself in January of 2016. That was the first court date. He denied the allegations and pled not guilty. The judge scheduled a hearing later in the month where Brittini and the other girl would have to testify. Then the judge would decide if the case should go to court.

The second court date was the day of the hearing, I didn't know what to expect. Our family stood together outside of the courtroom until we were called in. While we were standing there, I noticed my son and husband making a wall between where the girls were standing and who the guards were bringing in. I got a glimpse of my brother being taken into the courtroom. He was wearing an orange jumpsuit and his hands and feet were chained. I couldn't believe what I was seeing. My brother and I were so close growing up; what happened?! One of the hardest things I've ever had to do was walk into that courtroom. I didn't want to, but I needed to be there for Brittini... she was still my little girl. I couldn't focus on the fact that I felt frozen. With all the will power I had, I walked in to that room and took a seat. As I sat there, I listened to Brittini and the other girl testify to what happen to them. What I heard was disgusting. After about a half an hour, the judge said he had heard enough. There was enough reason for this case to go to court. It was a minor victory, but just the beginning of a long and grueling process.

Over the next couple of years, we had so many continuances and extensions. We just wanted to get it over with. No one seemed to care much about the victims. There was so much public attention over this case. Social media was going crazy talking about it. You see, my brother was a public-school teacher that was forced to resign over inappropriate conduct with the students a few years prior to this. Sadly, my kids went to this school. The school had ample evidence to prosecute him criminally but allowed him to resign instead. Unfortunately, this wasn't allowed to be brought up in Brittini's case. The court also decided to separate Brittini's and the other girl's case, which was in favor of Tom. Then, the person representing Brittini for the first two years was no longer on her case. The DA assigned a new prosecutor to handle her case weeks before her trial. He was very inexperienced but ambitious. He had a very limited amount of time to get up to speed on the case. All these things were sent to discourage us.

We were told statistically that there was less than a five percent chance of winning. We didn't look at the statistics because we serve a mighty God. Nothing is impossible with Him. There was a huge mountain in front of us... but our God is a mountain mover. After so many delays, Brittini finally got her day in court. The night before the trial began, Brittini and Seanny took their instruments to the court house to praise and worship God. They went to do battle. They knew as they lifted God up, He would lift them up.

Starting on November 14th, 2017, Brittini got to tell her story to a jury. I was called to testify about the layout of the house and a few other things, so I wasn't allowed in the courtroom except when I was called to the stand. So, I sat in the hallway and praised God. I had already prayed and declared God's Word over the situation... now I was thanking Him in advance for what He was about to do.

On Wednesday, November 15th, both lawyers gave their closing statements. My brother's lawyer started describing Brittini. She said something like, "Brittini was valedictorian of her class. She's been to multiple countries as a missionary. She's worked with girls that have been rescued from sex trafficking. She went to the Air Force Academy and excelled. She is no shrinking violet."

The jury deliberated less than two hours and came back with a verdict. As the jury walked by me, the Holy Spirit spoke to my heart. He said, "I hand selected each juror." Peace washed over me and confirmed what I already knew. The spokesperson for the jury stood up and started to read. The jury found my brother guilty on every single charge. The truth won. God, as always, was faithful.

After the trial, we talked about what the lawyer meant when she said, "Brittini is no shrinking violet." She was right, Brittini isn't a shrinking violet. She is a strong and accomplished woman. The lawyer was trying to say because Brittini is strong, she would have reported the abuse sooner. But just because you're strong doesn't mean that you're not sensitive or unsure at times. Brittini reminds me of Jesus. Jesus is the strongest, most powerful person this earth has ever seen. But Jesus cried when Lazarus died...even though He knew He would raise him from the dead. Jesus cried and sweat blood in the Garden of Gethsemane, even though He knew He would conquer death and be victorious. Jesus wept, not in defeat, but because He had a sensitive heart. Brittini is my violet... God's violet, His beautiful creation. She is not a shrinking violet. God has created each of us in a unique, special way.

During all of this, Alysha had one miscarriage, three surgeries, and gave birth to her daughter. Even though both of my girls were going through their own difficult times, they were there for each other. Alysha never missed one court date. Brittini was her big sister, a big part of her heart, and she loved her very much.

In March 2018, my brother was sentenced to eighteen to thirty-six years in prison and will be on probation for the rest of his life once he gets out. Although we won our case and were very grateful for this victory, it was still hard.

One thing we learned from this ordeal is that we have a very limited vision of the situations in our life. We were frustrated the case took so long. We felt let down when we got a new and inexperienced prosecutor. We were disappointed when we had to go through multiple jury selections. But the things that were trying to make us feel discouraged were really God lining things up on our behalf. Every setback in this case was for our benefit. We see a very small portion while God sees the whole picture. We never quit trusting Him or gave up, but at times, we saw things from a very small viewpoint.

We also learned that when things get shaky in our lives, our family gets stronger. Even though many people's words and actions hurt us, we had each other's backs. We are individuals that make a whole. When someone comes at one of us, they have to deal with all of us.

And most importantly, we learned the power of forgiveness. Forgiveness doesn't mean the crime is ok and forgotten about. Forgiveness means letting go of the bitterness and pain and allowing God to handle it. He can deal with our offenders in ways we never could. We trusted God with our pain, and He's healing us.

Six. The number six in the Bible symbolizes man. It represents human weakness and imperfection. Without

God, man can do unspeakable things and cause indescribable damage. Sin abounds in unthinkable ways when we live without God. Six days we spent in a courtroom over a three-year span. Each of those days left a mark on my family that changed us forever. Six times our love was burned even deeper for each other and God.

Chapter 7

$\mathcal{S}$even. Seven surgeries Alysha endure in a three-year time span. Seven times Alysha went under the knife. Seven times Alysha had to relinquish all control to a person she barely knew.

Surgery is to be cut open in the attempt to treat a problem or repair an injury. I feel surgery affects our mind as much as our body. There is a fear and a surrender that goes with surgery. You have to mentally prepare more than you do physically. It is quite the mind battle to decide whether or not to allow someone to put you unconscious, use knives and tools to cut you open, then explore the inside of you.

Alysha's first surgery was October 1st, 2015. It was a D&C, which stands for dilation and curettage. Alysha was pregnant and had been in the emergency room five times that week in the process of miscarrying. She was in so much pain and bleeding immensely. On Thursday September 30th, Alysha called me at the school where I was working. She was in a lot of pain and didn't know what to do. Her husband was at work at a relatively new job, so she didn't want him to leave before his shift ended. I told her to call her dad and have him take her to the ER. I would get there as soon as I could find someone to cover my class. This was her fifth visit to the emergency room. While she was there, Alysha passed the fetus. After giving her intravenous morphine, they sent her home. She had a follow-up appointment with her OBGYN on Friday October 1st. Her doctor reviewed her ultra-sound test and realized she hadn't passed all the tissue from the pregnancy. She contacted the hospital and made an appointment for Alysha to have D&C. Alysha went home after this and waited for the hospital to call her with an available time. Finally, about three hours later, she got the call from the hospital. Because of the delay, Chris was now home and able to take her. Chris was so upset and worried that Alysha focused on him. This was a blessing in disguise because Alysha wasn't focusing on how scared she was. At the hospital, she had to sign consent papers saying she understood the risks and benefits of this surgical procedure. Between the pain, uncertainty, and the loss, everything was just a blur. The procedure didn't take very long, and they sent her home late that night with some pain medication. Alysha felt so empty and broken inside. It had been an exhausting week in every way. She told me she was clinging to a thread of hope that her body was in the healing process. When your children are little, it's so hard to see them hurting. When they're adults, it doesn't get any easier.

Alysha was in a lot of pain and discomfort non-stop from her first surgery. The pain should have been lessening, but it wasn't. One of the doctors told her that her recovery was more mental than physical. She suggested going to a grief therapist. Alysha didn't go with that option. She knew there was something physically wrong, but no one believed her. Alysha called off work on October 30th, so she could rest. Her stomach pain was getting worse, and each step was excruciating. She called her doctor, and they said they could squeeze her in at their office later that day. Alysha saw a doctor that she had never seen before. The doctor, without running any tests, told Alysha that she believed she was pregnant and would send her for an ultrasound. Alysha insisted that she was not pregnant but refuses any pain medication just in case. A small seed of hope was planted by this doctor, and Chris and Alysha couldn't help but feel a little excited. Down deep, Alysha knew something was wrong, though. They went to the clinic to have the test done. It was so painful, it was almost unbearable. The tech assured them that Alysha was not pregnant... crushing the new hope that had just been planted. The tech told Alysha she needed to go back to the doctor to find out the results. As if the pain and mental torment weren't enough… let's just prolong all of this. Chris drove Alysha right back to the doctor's office, but they were at lunch. Alysha decided to wait because the pain was getting more intense. Back in the exam room, the doctor told Alysha that she is not pregnant, but there were some complications from the first D&C. This doctor had no idea how hurtful and hard her words were on Alysha that day. Evidentially, scar tissue had built up in her that wasn't allowing the blood to exit her body. So, it was just building up inside of her, causing the pain. The doctor tried to manually break through the scar tissue with an instrument that looked like a long fish hook. After two failed attempts, Alysha was writhing in pain. The doctor sent Alysha back to the emergency room for surgery. They did the procedure and kept her overnight. The next morning, the same doctor that saw Alysha the day before, walked into her room to check on her. She said to Alysha, "What are you going to dress your baby up as for Halloween?" Alysha almost couldn't speak. She told the doctor she was in the wrong room, and that she was the patient she saw yesterday and was told by her that her baby was gone. Chris was furious at this doctor's insensitivity. Alysha was just wiped out, physically and emotionally. On the way home from the hospital, Alysha asked Chris to stop at Kohls so she could get a normal pair of jeans. She had been wearing stretchy or maternity clothes because she was so bloated. She wanted to feel "normal" again and was trying to any way she could. Later that day, Alysha went to a friend's baby shower. She wanted to be happy and supportive... but deep down this was throwing salt on her wounds.

Alysha's third surgery wasn't even a month later. She was still having a lot of pain, so on November 13th I met her at the ER after work. The physician's assistant checked her out, ordered a shot of morphine, and discharged her with the diagnosis of indigestion. Alysha knew something was wrong, but no one would listen to her. Discouragement hung over her like a shadow. Her heart was broken over the baby she lost, and her mind was hurt that no one would believe her that something was wrong. Her body needed relief from the pain she was in. Three days later, Alysha was fevered, puking, and in a tremendous amount of pain. She had to go back to the doctor's office, and after taking a look at her they admitted her to the hospital. There, they put her on intravenous antibiotics for the infection and kept her five days. Every day, they told Alysha if she wasn't better by the next day, they were going to do exploratory surgery. And each day the doctor would pass it on to the next day and the next doctor. On Friday morning, November 20th, I came to visit Alysha early in the morning. They were in the process of discharging her. I took one look at her and went out to the desk to find the doctor. I was in full mother mode. If you've ever seen someone in this mode, you know to run immediately (smile). I found the doctor, and as respectfully as I could I said, "I'm not sure why you are releasing my daughter. She is in no better shape than when she came here. She is tossing and turning in pain. Something needs to be done." The doctor responded, "Well, nothing major is showing up on the tests. I believe the discomfort will go away in time. Exploratory surgery was suggested, but I don't like to do surgeries unless completely necessary." I looked that doctor in the eye and said, "Listen. With all due respect, I know my daughter and her body better than you do. I am not taking her home until you find out what is wrong and will help her." For about two minutes that doctor and I just started at each other... neither of us willing to be the one to break eye contact. Finally, the doctor said, "Ok, I'll take her down to surgery immediately." I waited for a few hours for Alysha to be brought back to her room. Before she arrived, the doctor came in to talk to me. She said, "You were right. Something was wrong. Alysha had endometriosis, scar tissue, and adhesions throughout her. Her ovary was adhered to her uterus, which was ripping with movement. We had to stitch her uterus because of the damage. We removed some of the endometriosis, but not all of it." I was grateful for the outcome, praying that everything would be able to heal now.

Alysha's fourth surgery was December 14th, 2017. She had scheduled this surgery with a different doctor to have the endometriosis removed. Her hope was that it would relieve the pain and help her to heal so she could try to conceive again. After the surgery, the doctor told her that she opened her up and saw no active endometriosis. She told Alysha to try some pelvic physical therapy and that there should be no problem with her conceiving and having a successful pregnancy. She released her the same day.

Time passed, and Alysha was still in pain. One day in January 2018, Alysha and I were walking at the gym. We talk about everything and figure out how to solve the world's problems. I told her to be in prayer for Bruce Bandel because he was on dialysis and not doing well. She responded, "If he needs a kidney, I'll give him one." I smiled and said, "Pray about it before you make a decision like that." Down deep I knew God was working on her heart. No normal person just decides to donate a kidney on a whim. I didn't say anything else, knowing that something special was taking place.

In March 2018, she found out her and Chris were expecting again. She couldn't have contained her excitement if she tried. She started planning for this baby immediately. On an especially warm and sunny spring day in April, her and I were sitting on my porch swinging and talking. Bruce pulled into our driveway to see Sean but stopped to visit with us on the porch first. Out of the blue, Alysha says, "Bruce, I'm pregnant and my baby is due in November. But if you still need a kidney by the beginning of 2019, I'll donate one for you." Bruce got a little teary. He thanked Alysha for the incredible gesture, but told her he'd have his miracle by the end of the year. The Holy Spirit came over me, and I said, "Bruce, don't limit your miracle by putting God in a box. Jesus used all different kinds of methods to heal." I asked him if I could pray with him. So, Alysha, Bruce, and I joined hands and prayed. I declared God's Word over Bruce, and asked God to fill Bruce with His wisdom and knowledge." It's always good when God's family gets together.

A few weeks later, Alysha started having another miscarriage. Her body was fighting the process with all it had. But by May 2nd, she was fevered and double over in pain. The doctor told Alysha to go to the ER. When Chris came home, they dropped Mia off at my house and headed to the hospital. They wanted to send Alysha home and have her schedule a D&C with her doctor when it was convenient for them. She insisted that they keep her and do the surgery as soon as possible. She couldn't understand why they would delay it, especially since she was fevered and in pain. They agreed to keep her overnight and do the procedure the next morning at 5:30 a.m. This would be her fifth surgery. Alysha was just exhausted from literally fighting with her doctors' office that whole week to take care of her. To top it all off, Alysha felt bad that she was in the hospital and not feeling well enough to take a meal to a family friend. Alysha looked forward to Thursdays, so that she could visit with Ed and Linda and take them a meal. Linda was in her last stages of cancer, so Alysha knew their time together was limited and precious. Alysha felt like her heart was shattering into a thousand pieces.

Alysha's sixth surgery was to happen on July 5th, 2018. She found a doctor that specialized in endometriosis. Alysha knew there was still something not right going on inside her body. This doctor agreed to do surgery to see what was going on. Thankfully, there was a cancellation, and Alysha's surgery got moved up to June 4th. Days before this surgery, Alysha was walking with Mia at the park and saw Rachel, Bruce's daughter. Alysha told her we were still praying for her dad, and after this next surgery, if she were able to, she wanted to start the screening process for kidney donation. Rachel thanked her and said they had faith that her dad would be receiving his miracle soon. On June 4, Alysha went in for surgery. The doctor removed a lot of endometriosis that the previous surgery had missed just six months ago. The doctor also removed Alysha's tubes, making a normal pregnancy impossible. Although this broke Alysha's heart, she was relieved she wouldn't have to go through another miscarriage. She said her heart and body couldn't handle another one.

From this doctor's perspective, Alysha was cleared to begin the donor screening process—surgery seven. This was different from all the other surgeries. This was a surgery Alysha decided to do. This was a surgery that was going to bring life... not death. This surgery would prove that Alysha's body could still give life in other ways. This surgery was based completely and totally on love.

Seven. In a three-year span, Alysha would have seven surgeries. Seven is the number of completeness. It's the number of divine perfection. It had just begun.

Chapter 8

So, here I am... still sitting in my rocking chair reflecting on everything that's happened the past few years to get us to this point. I stand amazed at how God worked everything out for our good and loved us through it all. I look at the clock. Alysha would still be in surgery at this point.

I start thinking about some of the things Alysha has said and done over the past few months. When she first learned that she was a candidate to be a donor, she said to me, "Mom, you know how jealous I've been of you and Brittini over the years because of how thin you both are?" I stopped her immediately and said, "You are blessed to be so curvy and beautiful." She interrupts me and continues, "I finally realized God made me this way for a reason. You and Brittini have always been so skinny and haven't weighed enough to donate blood, let alone a kidney. Thick thighs save lives." Oh my... only Alysha would come up with a slogan like that.

I thought of all the negative comments Alysha endured, especially the week leading up to the surgery. Satan used so many people to try to instill fear and stop her from going through with it. They wanted her to make sure she was aware of all the risks this surgery entailed. They were clueless compared to her. She went through months and months of information about all that would happen. People even called her selfish. They said she was putting herself before her family. She told me the more criticism she heard, the more she leaned on the Lord. The joy of the Lord really was her strength. I always wanted to teach my kids to have "bulldog" faith. The kind of faith that grabbed onto what the Lord said and wouldn't let go for anything. She said every time someone would speak fear into her life, God would bring the twenty-third Psalm to her mind. She would hear it down in her heart, "He restores my soul, even though I walk through the valley of the shadow of death, I will fear no evil, for He is with me. He anoints my head with oil, my cup overflows (verse 3-5)." The Word of God is alive and active... "sharper than any two-edged sword" (Hebrews 4:12). You are dangerous to the Devil when the Word of God is on your lips. That's why he tries so hard to distract you and get you to fear.

As she was leaving for the hospital this morning, she stopped and really looked at the sign at the foot of the steps in my hallway. It says, "The Will of God will never take you where the Grace of God will not protect you." She said it was like God was talking to her and reassuring her that He was taking every step with her. She knew if God was for her, who could be against her?

Then I thought of myself. As her mother, I was so proud of her... yet I wanted to take her place. But she's an adult now, and this is what she felt called to do. This was her path to walk, not mine. I started praying and declaring God's Word over her... and I realized something. I've had two children healed of cancer, won impossible trials, have had supernatural protection, and more miracles than I can list. I no longer want to just defeat Satan... I want to make a public spectacle of him like Jesus did in Colossians 2:15. I'm no longer satisfied with just winning... I want him to be revealed for the pathetic loser that he is. Because of what Jesus accomplished at the cross, we are more than conquerors. I start praising and worshipping Jesus just at the thought of this. I don't care how undignified I was being... Jesus was worthy of it. He is the King of kings, our Healer, our Comforter, and we are His. I couldn't help but rejoice at how He was working in all our lives.

I look over at my flowers. What a wonderful reminder of how God can take dirty little seeds and turn them into something beautiful. Aren't we like that? A dirty little speck that God transforms into something beautiful, and that beauty spills out onto others... showing God's handiwork.

Chris is good about keeping us informed. Alysha went into surgery around 7:00 a.m., and Chris texted or called almost every hour with updates. Finally, a little after noon, Chris called and said Alysha was out of surgery and everything went well. He said he wouldn't be allowed to see her for a while yet. I raised my hands and thanked God for His goodness and faithfulness. I want to call Alysha so bad over the next few hours, but I knew she was too loopy and wouldn't know what she was saying... let alone remember the call. I ask Chris how Bruce is doing, but he said he hasn't heard any news on him yet.

What seemed like an eternity wait to hear from Alysha—okay, so it was only a few hours—finally happened. She called to talk to us on FaceTime later that evening. You could tell she was in some pain and very uncomfortable. She said she was doing okay, but we decided to wait until the next day to visit.

So, very early the next day, Sean and I left to go see our daughter. Driving to Pittsburgh has never been an enjoyable ride for us... the traffic is usually horrendous and causes the travel time to be three times longer than it should be. But because it was a weekend and early, we made good time. When we arrived in Alysha's room, she was struggling with the pain. I whispered to Sean that we weren't going to stay long because Alysha needed her rest. I asked her how everything went, and she said, "I feel like I got hit by a truck. Not some little S-10 truck, but by a big Mac truck. The nerve block was the worst part of it. I'd rather have my other kidney taken out than have to go through that again." She proceeded to tell us that when she woke up in recovery she was in a tremendous amount of pain. The nurse told her that her incision was lower and longer than initially expected so the nerve block was not helping with that pain. Her incision was supposed to be two inches but ended up being six inches. "I also kept asking for ice; my mouth was so dry. I had to wait in recovery for more than five hours before I could come to my room and have some. Although I didn't talk to them, I saw Bruce's wife and daughter in recovery. He was two beds down from me. The nurses weren't allowed to give me updates on Bruce, but his family appeared happy so I guess that was a good sign. Right before they brought me up to my room, a nurse whispered in my ear that Bruce was doing well. I was so happy to hear that. I got hiccups in the elevator on my way up to my room... they lasted like an hour. Each one caused such incredible pain. Plus, you know how ridiculous I sound when I get hiccups. The nurses couldn't help but laugh at me no matter how hard they tried not to. This caused me to laugh, which only caused more pain. Oh well, they say laughter is the best medicine. I didn't sleep very well. The nurses had to give me a blood thinner shot every six hours and check my vitals often. Plus, the IV machine would randomly beep. So, it was difficult to rest. I was excited to see you all this morning, so I tried to get cleaned up. After a minute or two of standing, I was completely exhausted. So, I may smell like medicine. Pastor Nate and Joie sent me flowers, aren't they beautiful? Oh, and by the way, I'm wearing the green living donor t-shirt you bought me… it was a big hit with the doctor and nurses." The front of her shirt said, "Who Wouldn't Want A Piece of This?"

Alright, Alysha was definitely wiped out and tired. She was rambling on and on and could barely keep her eyes open. It was sad and funny at the same time. I gave Sean a look that said we weren't staying much longer. I gave her a hug and kiss and told her we were so proud of her and loved her very much. I told her to FaceTime us later after she got some sleep. As I looked at Alysha lying in her hospital bed, I was looking at an extension of Jesus. The sacrifice she made for another human was straight from the heart of God.

Then we went to visit Bruce who was just across the hall from her. He was sitting up in a chair, chatting with his nurse. I couldn't get over how good he looked. He had great color and looked well rested. He told us that he slept five hours straight, which is the best sleep he had in a long time. He also said that he had already walked fourteen laps around his unit and was feeling good. His counts were improving by leaps and bounds and he was going to the bathroom frequently. He was in great spirits and praising God. Bruce got his miracle. Maybe not the way he had hoped for, but he got one none the less.

Chapter 9

For the next eight weeks, Alysha and her family stayed with us off and on. Chris worked, and Alysha wasn't allowed to pick up more than ten pounds. Her little girl weighed over twenty, so picking her up was out of the question. We had fun watching Christmas movies, eating, and visiting. There wasn't much else Alysha could do at first, so we made the best of it. Alysha and I had a lot of time to talk during her recovery. I told her I was praying that God miraculously gives her a new kidney. Her response was, "I don't need it, but if God gives me another one, I'll just find someone else to donate it to. I want God to know He can always count on me."

Alysha proceeds to tell me, "You know, Mom, you're the one that planted the seed in me to donate a kidney."

"How in the world do you figure that?"

"Well," she continues, "you always said, 'I love you so much I'd give you my kidney.' Even if someone made you mad or upset, you would say, 'I love them so much, I'd still give them a kidney.' So, you see, I always equated donating a kidney with love. You always said words are powerful. Look what you planted."

I never realized how much I said that or what an impact it made on my kids. God knew from the beginning what was going to happen, and I guess I just called it out (smile).

I remember the first time she showed me her scar... it was bigger than I expected. She said the size didn't bother her, it was a reminder. I told her scars are a sign that you lived and survived, that God's love and grace overcame the attack against you. It's a special beauty mark.

The week before Christmas, Bruce and his wife, Vicky, invited our whole family over for a special meal. Unfortunately, Brittini and her family were in Colorado, so they couldn't come. But the rest of us were able to go, including Seanny. They had their house all decked out for the holidays, and their table looked like it had been professionally set and decorated. Bruce and Vicky told Alysha she looked good and asked her how she was doing. By this point, Alysha was nearly 100% recovered and doing wonderful. Bruce said his counts were back to normal and he, too, was doing great. He said he couldn't remember a time when he had more energy.

As we sat down together to have this wonderful meal, Bruce said a prayer. My heart was overwhelmed by the love and tenderness that filled the room. I heard God speak in my spirit, "This is the way My family is supposed to act." Tears filled my eyes as I looked around the table at all these people who are so dear to me. I looked at the delicious food set before me. Then I thought of what God did to get us to this point.

God sent His one and only Son to this earth to be born in a manger. He deserved a palace but got a barn. A cold, smelly, dirty barn. That was because He was a gift to everyone. If He was born in a palace, only the rich and royals could have seen Him. But God loved every single person and placed Him where everyone would have access to Him. That was only part of the gift. Thirty-three years later was when the ultimate sacrifice would be made. That's when Jesus would willingly lay down His life to die for us. He voluntarily was tortured for us. He was whipped and beat until He didn't even look human. He literally looked like a raw piece of meat. He had thorns shoved into His head. People ripped the beard right off His face. He was mocked and ridiculed. He was nailed to a tree. When I asked Jesus how He could do this, He spoke to my spirit and said, "That's what love does... it gives."

And I saw it. Love has to give, period. It says in John 3:16, "For God so loved the world that He gave..." God loved, so He gave. As His children, it's in our spiritual DNA to give. We see a need, we help meet it. The world should know us by our love...it should draw them into the family of God. Christians should have the most radical love and generosity this world has ever seen. We should take after our Father.

As I look across the table at my daughter, I see Jesus's love shining in her eyes. Satan tried to break her in so many different ways. He lost. Her wounds made her more sensitive to other people that are hurting. Her battles made her realize that God was faithful and would never leave her or forsake her. Her trials showed her that problems are temporary... but love is eternal. Alysha not only gave Bruce the gift of life, but she gave his family back their husband, father, and grandfather. Love has such a ripple effect.

I look over at Bruce. Life is just radiating out of him. I smile and say, "Bruce, just so you know I'm claiming Psalm 91 over you, 'With long life will God satisfy you and show you His salvation.' Enjoy life with your family and get out there and win as many souls as possible with the extra years God is giving you."

He smiles his ornery smile and says, "That's my plan."

Some may think this is the end of our story. But really, God is just getting started. It has just begun...

Epilogue

Once upon a time, way back in 1990, God brought together a most beautiful princess and a handsome prince. They were strong and stubborn. They loved each other so very much that the Lord placed a call on their lives to raise up a royal family. God looked down from Heaven and smiled, "They are kind, loving, relentless, and passionate. They will rise victorious in all things and bring glory to My name." This troubled the Devil. He thought to himself, *I must break them.*

The Lord gave the prince and princess two daughters and a son. He entrusted them to raise these children to be warriors for Him. Satan attacked the young royal family with his very best. When the young son was only three years old, he was diagnosed with cancer. The prince's job was very dangerous and stressful, and money was tight. Meanwhile, the princess's brother preyed on the oldest daughter while the princess cared for her son who was fighting for his life in the hospital. Satan made their world miserable and cold, but God didn't allow him to have the final word. Behind the scenes, God was aligning every-thing just right for them. He was healing them in every area that was wounded. The family, truly warriors at heart, rose victorious and proclaimed God's love throughout the land. The prince and princess led by example and taught their children the ways of the Lord. They instilled in them many talents, but most importantly they ingrained a bulldog faith and a heart for God's people.

Growing up, I always had a great anticipation to see the Lord unfold a fairytale-like story in my life; after all, I am a daughter of the royal family. I fell fast and hard in love with my own prince, Christopher, and we got mar-ried after dating for only six months. Around this time, I began hearing the phrase, "You're crazy," more and more. I wonder why? Since my youth, I knew in my heart that I wanted to be a wife and mother. I wanted a big family with lots and lots of kids. After much heartache and pain with the loss of our first two pregnancies, the Lord blessed us with our rainbow baby, Amelia Rae. Our hearts rejoiced. I often told Christopher that our love was going to change the world. Amelia is our love, and she is going to change the world.

Our daughter has brought us so much joy. Every time I look at her, I am reminded that God is still in the business of doing miracles. We decided after Amelia's first birthday I would undergo surgery once again in hopes of continuing to grow our family. I was able to get pregnant again, but after only ten short weeks, I had my third miscarriage. The loss of our son was followed by two more surgeries and the loss of my ability to have more children. My heart broke like it never had before. I got alone with the Lord and told Him in order to begin to heal, I needed to know He could still use my body to produce life like it was created to do. I needed to know God would still grow our family.

Throughout my childhood, I heard that God doesn't call the qualified, He qualifies the called. God revealed Himself to me, gave me a peace that passes all understanding, and showed me that each of my pregnancies gave me a unique and beautiful gift. He helped me find strength in Him. He restored my soul. A dear friend of the family was dealing with kidney disease and was faithfully believing God for a miracle. God allowed me to be a part of his miracle. As I began testing to become a living donor, I heard I was crazy more times than I can count. The Lord taught me that His joy is truly my strength. He filled me with laughter. He showed me that in giving my joy is complete. The timing was all a little bittersweet, I ended up donating my kidney the same week that should have been my due date with my son. But God showed me that my treasures are not lost, they are stored up in Heaven where

I will one day get to hold my children and lavish my love upon them. What a grand reunion that will be!

Why would anybody donate a kidney? Maybe I am just a little bit crazy, but mostly because God placed that call on my life. As a child, my mom would often use the expression "I love you so much I'd give a kidney for you." I grew up believing if you love someone, you give them a kidney. I have a new perspective in life. God has shown me it's not about what you lose – it's about what you gain in the process. The day after my surgery, Bruce's son and daughter-in-law, Ryan and Julia, came to visit me. I felt like I got hit by a bus, and I knew I had weeks of recovery in front of me. Ryan and Julia brought me flowers, and by the end of the night, so did Vicky and Rachel, along with Bruce's brother and his wife. As I looked over my room, which was beginning to look like a floral shop, I saw that God has given me a family-in-love in the Bandels. Their visit brought me so much joy, even in my pain and drugged state. I marvel at God's grand design. Even a gift as simple as the flowers, He brought me joy, showed His beauty, and masked the stink of not being able to shower for two days in the hospital. God showed me that in giving my kidney, I gave Vicky back her husband, Ryan and Rachel back their father, Bruce's siblings back their brother, and the grandkids more time with their grandfather. This simple act of obedience was changing lives, including mine. There is nothing special about me. My kidney wasn't the Holy Grail of kidneys (however, I hear its now filtering some serious amounts of urine). It was just simply that the Lord called, and I answered. I have seen firsthand that God works together all things—the good, bad, and ugly— for our good.

So, what's next? To be honest, I'm not completely sure. I know I'm looking forward to our next adventure. God has been good to me, much better than I deserve. My husband and I hope to open our home to fostering or adopting in the years to come. I know that no matter what may come our way, with God and each other, we always will rise victorious.

I hope my story touched your heart and encouraged you for your own journey. While I am quick to say I don't have all the answers, I am glad to know the One who does. I am living proof that God makes beauty from ashes and is still in the business of working miracles.

Love,
Alysha Rae

The Invitation

⁓

*A*re you a part of God's family? Would you like to be? If so, then repeat after me:

Dear God, thank You for sending Your Son, Jesus, to the earth for me. I confess that Jesus is the Son of God and that He died on the cross in my place to pay for the punishment of my sins. I believe that He rose from the dead, victorious over sin and death. I believe that Jesus is now in Heaven, sitting at the right hand of God, reigning as the King of kings and Lord of lords. I ask You, Jesus, to forgive me of all my sins. I receive Your forgiveness and grace. I ask You, Jesus, to be my Lord and Savior and to come into my heart.

If you prayed this prayer... CONGRATULATIONS! All the angels in heaven are rejoicing for you. You are now a child of the Almighty God. Your name is written in the Book of Life, and your eternity is sealed in Heaven. You get to spend forever with God and His family in His kingdom, where it is beautiful, amazing, and fun. Nothing – nothing – will separate you from His love.

It is important now to find a Bible-believing, Holy Spirit-filled church that is full of God's love and will help you grow. Take time to read the Bible and get to know your God. He will never quit amazing you or loving you. People, even Christians, may let you down... but God never will. The choice is yours. What are you going to do?

Tracey is a Pastor and the author of two other books:

"And Then...God Showed Me His Love" and "Muscle Up."

If you would like to contact Tracey for prayer or for a speaking engagement, the email address is:

AbbasREMNANT@aim.com

Please feel free to visit her web-page at:

www.godshowedmehislove.com

CPSIA information can be obtained
at www.ICGtesting.com
Printed in the USA
BVHW082318040919
557597BV00011B/477/P